Broken Grace at Low Tide

Broken Grace at Low Tide

Poems by

Sally Stewart Mohney

Cover design by Shay Culligan
Cover image, "Sand and Sea," courtesy of Frances Roosevelt
Author photo by Ashley Mohney Eggleston

ISBN: 978-1-63980-655-3

Kelsay Books
502 South 1040 East, A-119
American Fork, Utah 84003
Kelsaybooks.com

for my husband
for our harbor

Acknowledgments

I'm grateful to be included in the following:

Acumen Literary Journal, London: "Nocturne in the Barrow Orchard"

Broad River Review: "Wearing my Pale Life," Ron Rash Award Finalist

Georgia Poetry Society Reach of Song Anthology: "Watching your daughter drink Charleston fog," First Place in Member Excellence Poetry Award

San Pedro River Review: "Flooded Landscape with Lost Totems," "Notes from Your Mother's Edge"

STILL: The Journal: "After baptism: the quickening"

A very special thanks to Katie Chaple and her Poetry@Tech workshop and to Karen Paul Holmes's Side Door workshop.

Contents

Broken Grace
at Low Tide

Violet cloud surges
above a vague gray sea.

The sound of our screen
door shuddering.

You lit my mind like a wick—
now the wick is buried in wax.

Nothing left on the beach
except
winter mist
and a skein of fish.

A lone heron lands
in cordgrass
off the black bank.

Silent lit ship slides by.

Stars that never
blink or beckon.

please open the sky

Clouds lift like spirits

off long cumulus bank—
migrating purple.

Wind-christened
trees, heave and cry
ruach.

Above the Barren River,
sudden sandhills—

a herd of crane colts
rise,

their rolling cries
leave you behind

rudderless.

Nocturne in the Barrow Orchard

Under a blood moon
disquiet in the sourwood copse:

one forgotten lamp—

a barn owl

in a chalk-plumed cassock.
His cream face—
a crumpled camellia.

In your head, he watches
waits, whinging like a conjured clock.

do not listen

Flooded Landscape with Lost Totems

White oaks quake and dead chestnuts roll
on the Chattahoochee bottom. One copper
Cooper's hawk pecks each cabin window—
mewling, flashing like lightning.

Black snake ropes around
your porch posts as the river
crests at the moment
of blinking.

A doe wades upland through the brush
with a split tongue. The rutting roan
buck waits on the other side.

When will the wind lie down?

How sage water is at peace flowing high by the old white praise house

Morning storm edges onto Coffin Point Road.
Hardtack clouds hover above the cemetery, as a river
jail inmate stops mowing around standing stones.
A lost white tail doe searches for the lay of the land.

Alzina's truck stop—a sheet metal stand.
Among the early faces, my palms—damp
dogwood leaves. She slides me eggs on a warm
metal tray. Amen-colored sun burns off fatal fog.

I am a lost old creek drinking a clear jar

After baptism: the quickening

Your chilled feet
rest one on top
of the other.
Fingers cover
your face.

Stream scent—
pure snowmelt.

You take
a swallow
and begin

again.

Unhappen

Light leaches through the window—
lambent, you are confined to two rooms.

Lightning lashes through your back,
fire threads its way through the vertebrae.

Pieces of fallen grace land in another realm

after breaking through burning
bushes and soaring over a stone wall

of silver silence.

Wearing my pale life

as a loose linen robe—waiting, wonting
while broken in bed, steps away
from the threatening staircase.

Soon able to sit, spine-still,
and peer out
the bay window
at the aftermath: one
bereft gray hydrangea, once
robust with blue.

Finally, first steps:
one sudden afternoon
you lead me gingerly
to the old bridge

over flat ground
under copper
turning trees
past abundant
overgrown laurel vine

reaching for us—

I cling to your
waxed coat elbow.

Then we tread
over splintered planks
hold
the wrought rail
in our cold palms

as hazel water
courses beneath.

Then home
to a fall fire—
lantern to light
our feet into another
Season.

You knew I needed to witness
my river again.

Self-portrait in bone, leather, horn

Relics from the lost season—
talismans or totems?

Mounted in the closet
with fog-colored walls:

needle-bone earrings
leather belt in a snake-curl
white horn cuff
that once encircled your wrist—

now overwrought, weighted.

Hidden inside a drawer beneath:

ivory tooth hanging off of a
strange, strangled necklace—
silver, hammered—

trapped inside of a knotted
net scarf.

And there is something else
you discover—

don't give it a name

The Reclusive Landscape

I want to learn how
to walk
Again.

Wend through the ballast stone
lanes and mews of the old
district. Witness houses
grow a silver patina—
while window boxes thrive.

The full barrow of trailing ivy
and red cyclamen hearts

next to the zinc watering can.

As crepe myrtles slowly learn
how to stretch and unfold,
instead I am lost

in a thousand-acre sleep.

After the quake

trees speak before
houses do. Bare-boned
crepes on upheaved
cobble. Broken
limbs litter the lane—
wrought gates
swing off post.

Silent houses suffer

shattered piazzas
slumped gables
ragged eaves.

Stern copper lamps witness
haint blue ceilings
stained with silt.
Collapsed balusters—
the color of dusk.

Sullen hinges hang
off splintered shutters.

Creeping fig still quietly weaves
jade over cracked tombstones.

Indigo tides, trembling—
soon hushed. Lone

hound seeks the river.

At the corner of church and water

*'August Ladies' were impoverished grand dames of old Charleston
who couldn't escape summer plagues. They emerged only in the
dark evenings.*

When I become

a woman of
August

I will set down my bone
cup, snuff the candle
with old silver

and float down Water
Street in a
broderie anglaise gown.

Lay in the church garden
over white stones—

lap full of lace—

under pale relics of clouds

If I could ever speak to you again

I would mention how the sturdy green
boxwood was underplanted with white
cyclamen hearts on Queen Street.

Just as I underplanted you, as pale
pansies, under your great

green cypress.

Watching your daughter drink Charleston Fog

under bay laurel branches
at a whitewashed table

on the corner of Meeting
& Queen.

Your smile mirrored
in her dark glasses.

Her wide white cup—
Earl Grey and lavender.

You hover over lemon toast and know
you will never see her again—
like this.

You are seized
trying to freeze

the moment

but know that you'll have to let her go

again

I wish I was here

Remember when we wore kaftans

and drank dark coffee
on the country terrace overlooking
the lake with migratory geese?

You said coffee tasted better
in the city
with Catskills water.

Then we drank cava on the balcony
overlooking the Alboran Sea.
You rolled a cigarette
and burnt a perfect
hole in your coral
kaftan.

Now I wear a black one
with bitter coffee and news
and wonder
where you are.

The last time we met
you cupped your palm
over your ear
like a conch.

Your Silence since—
a sour shell's breath
in my ear

Notes from your Mother's Edge

You are left
lost in your mother's
Manhattan apartment—
the one on the 11th floor
with the mirrored wall
which reflected the river.

Once, you saw her sepia silhouette
at the plate-glass window
looking over strange water—
her back to you. Water

you had never seen.

But you found her.

You were born haunted,
she said.

She disappeared at the end of May.

Left her bone china cup, half-full
of rosehip tea, in the eau de nil room
with ghost-white branches
stretching around the walls—

her smoke in your hair.

Bloomsbury, 1978

Remember when you left London

that raw October
to fly back to Tel Aviv?

After you disappeared
on the Underground to Heathrow,
I crossed the road to Russell Square.

I lay on leaves under lit lime trees

in my blue loden coat
and Chelsea boots—a fallen

Alice in Wonderland.

I returned to my Georgian office

rolled, lit a Rothmans and slid
my typewriter roller to the left.

North of Battersea Bridge

after James McNeill Whistler

The Thames a gray note—an arrangement in blue
and silver. Plane trees etch the cinder sky. Black
lamp posts burn, cobbles steam. Longboats are left
moored under blank oriel windows. The river is draped

by a tattered cape of fog. As the color of the air shifts,
stains—the embankment suddenly swells

with a sepia tide of images: men in top hats
and waistcoats, women in cloaks with parasols—
children in caps, running. The buckle-cadence
of a horse carriage. Hushed, they soon turn

into lost smoke.

I still think about you

in that Salamanca café
off of Jorge Juan.

Your drinking kir
in the morning.
Your wild claims,
your wild husband.

No warning
your falling.

Your hair always a dark
halo above your head.

With My Father, Missing the Second Train

Remember when we took the train from Cordele
after the wake?

Dark pecan groves flanked the Blackshear
banks, one lone cypress in the river.

Venetian blinds clicked against the windows

and a yellowed apron of Edward Hopper
light settled on our backs.

After arriving in the station, you sat—

a mangrove statue on a cement bench—
as if keeping it from flying away.

Dusk paints us
    broken in half

On the Greyhound Leaving Des Moines

I sit next to a young woman
with a lost face, wearing
a bedspread. She has pewter eyes.

When I smile and ask where she's from,
she tilts her head. *I'm a Muskogee Creek.*
Her lap shelters sage stones.

Across the aisle is a middle-aged man
with waxed hair and sunglasses. He
looks familiar—our ex-accountant?
Insurance agent, something mutual?
Should I say, *Mr. Norberg? Vic?*
But he is busy searching out
the window, as if for a lost son.
Trembling, he checks his Casio watch.

Rescuing? Or running away.

I peer out the glass as the low rye banks
of I-80 spool by, and my mind harkens back
to the dull sour pond outside our honeymoon
motel in Dothan.

There is a gray stray rain.

Three states away in Sevier County,
quaking aspens are lit like candles.

Childhood

i. Wearing that army green
duffel coat, the scratchy
woolen jacket with the bucket
hood that never fully covered

my head—stopped short
of my crown. When it drizzled
I walked with water in my eyes,
coat smelling like my lost dog.

ii. It was too tight, too hot.
My mother struggled to thread
the wooden toggles up to my throat.

iii. So one purple day, I decided
to peel it off slowly—a tear
in one shoulder, a frayed hem.

I held my head straight, didn't
look down, and ferried

Forward

as myself.

All Saints Chapel
Charleston County, August, 1965

Yellow yawns, hollow stares.
Overhead, the paddle fan moans.
Wilted white sprays of flowers
behind the polished casket.
We are hushed like smoke.

The minister begins to drone on
about 'Our Father' and a new
body and a risen life.

My aunt faints, falls into the aisle—
a dark-suited deacon pulls her up by tweed
arms and places her back in the pew.
Her stale breath blooms behind me.

There is a slight stir. My throat—
as dry as a communion wafer.

Sitting on the shelf next to the prayer
book is the small red pencil burrowed
into a hole. I draw a family under a tree,
smiling into outer space—dolls
holding out empty hands.

My brother, in a tight suit and waxed
crewcut, flips his program over, grabs
a fountain pen from Grandmother's purse
and scrawls war planes with lines shooting
down to land, leaving inky holes where
soldiers' hearts should be. He makes low
rat tat tat and *boom* sounds.

Grandmother can't hear and stares ahead
in a black pillbox hat with a net over her eyes.
Father, with a pale face and wicked-back hair,
takes the pen away and slides it into his pocket.

Last Easter, my brother tried to be an acolyte
in a white ghost gown, carrying the cross
down the aisle while his shoulders shook.

Afterwards, Mother hugged my brother,
as an arch deacon clapped my father's arms.

You were a wonderful crucifer, she smiled,
crouching down in her pink melton cape.
Your mother held a glove on his cheek
and reached out a wing to gather me in.

Suddenly we all stand to sing the hymn,
"As Longs the Deer for Cooling Streams."

I peer outside the tall window—my mother is not
trapped inside that box but perched

    in the white

        river birch tree.

Requiem with Winter Driftwood

Ferrying my parents over the black Santee River and through the forest, we return to the Hammock Coast. I steal a peek in my rearview mirror, afraid they may vanish.

My mother looks out the window with a sere smile, taking in the marsh and pines as if for the first or final time. Shivering in her black tea length dress, her hair is a golden halo.

My father, in his charcoal gray suit, gazes ahead as if reading the newspaper or accepting a sentence. I sense a world-weary sigh.

Our old cottage—egret-white, perched on a swell of aged groundsel—looms ahead, now shuttered, silent. When we enter the pine living room, the dark galley kitchen in the corner smells of smoke. My mother hovers there for a minute—fingers fluttering— and I can almost hear her say, *a labor of love.* Her endless evening suppers, or is she remembering her lost life?

She will want candles, so I take the driftwood lanterns out to the porch. After I light the hurricanes with wooden matches from the sill, we settle in rockers and wait. Wordlessly, we watch pelicans— three gray flags—flap past.

Suddenly my father sheds his coat and walks out the screened door, white hair aloft in the breeze, shirt tails flapping, as if to take flight. Studying the sea as if it would reclaim him. My mother joins him at the rail—her plight of troth—and takes his elbow.

I carry the guttering lamps to join them, *bearing witness.*

While lambent
in her last bed

she watched me
with her wise brown
unblinking eyes—

unwavering, unfaltering
unnerving.

Now I know it was more
than a Parkinson's stare,
more than a mask.

She studied my face—
my now wise brown eyes—

because she might never see me again.

Winter Solstice

As you ended

I said, please don't
haunt me.

So, you've been silent
Ever Since.

Until overnight

the forgotten
Forsythia
rises beneath
the ghost hemlock

lifts a bright
Yellow flag—

your silent
harbinger—

the spring
thaw has finally

arrived.

Peonies, Again

for my husband

Today, both
our mother's
bushes

erupted in bloom.

Buried and planted one May—
now rising in another May.

Pink and white heads bow

in respect, of
what once
was

now beyond.

Sudden Peonies

for my mother

The shocking shaggy heads
are back, I forgot yours was white.

I had to prop it up properly
with your cane and

stove you up
like old times.

Aubade, Retiro Park

Chestnut trees—their plump glossy fruit
rests on a pedestal, under a Spanish king's
statue. *There was a tree at my bus stop*
and we would pull the shells apart, you say.

Under cypresses, we sit to watch kindergartners—
a row of ducklings—hold a rope to wend around
the pond. When set free, the boys gather nuts
in their shirt hems while the girls sit down in a circle,
as hushed as nuns.

The elders meet—a flowing Tai Chi with swords—
first moving sculpture,
then silent poses.

In front of the Cristal Palace—a Lone
black swan—widow, warrior? Lifts her neck
high, cries a soft plea.

Can't we hide inside?
Forget winter, death.
The Palace has spare
elegant bones. High
ceilings, lots of space.

Your profile the same as when
you were nineteen—china blue eyes,
noble nose.

The fallen golden cups of plane trees.

It is autumn. We are 67. At ease
with daily grace—I can never lose

the spokes of sun striking
your handsome face.

About the Author

Sally Stewart Mohney graduated from the University of North Carolina-Chapel Hill Honors Program in Writing and has taken graduate courses at the University of Iowa Writers' Workshop.

She is the recipient of the Jesse Rehder Writing Prize from UNC Chapel Hill, as well as two First Prize Awards in Excellence and the Mnemosyne Award from the Georgia Poetry Society. She is a James Applewhite Award and a Ron Rash Award finalist. Twice she has been nominated for Georgia Author of the Year in Poetry.

Her publications include *eventide* (Kelsay Books, 2020), *A Piece of Calm* (Finishing Line Press, 2014), and *pale blue mercy* (Main Street Rag, Author's Choice Series, 2013). Her collection *Low Country, High Water* (Texas Review Press, 2016) won the Southern Poetry Anthology Prize: North Carolina. Her work has appeared in *Acumen Literary Journal—London, Atlanta Journal & Constitution, Charlotte Observer, Cortland Review, James Dickey Review, North Carolina Literary Review, San Pedro River Review, Verse Daily, WinningWriters.com,* and elsewhere. Mohney's work has been anthologized and featured in galleries and exhibitions.

She lives on the Charleston harbor.

www.ingramcontent.com/pod-product-compliance
Lightning Source LLC
Chambersburg PA
CBHW031008090426
42737CB00008B/738